ABC Vision

A simple guide on the ABCs of Success and how to live the life you want to lead!

Dr. Wilson L. Triviño

Aura Free Press

Copyright © 2015 by Dr. Wilson Lubin Triviño

All rights reserved. No part of this book may be used or reproduced in any manner whatsoever without prior written consent of the author, except as provided by the United States of American copyright law.

Published by Aura Free Press, Marietta, Georgia USA

ISBN-10: 097432601
ISBN-13: 978-0-9743226-0-5

DEDICATION

To my family:

My mami and papi – Lubin and Aura Triviño- who sacrificed it all for me to have access to the American dream and a world of opportunity.

My brothers: David, Daniel, and Miguel Triviño- my constant supporters.

More importantly to the newest Triviños, my nieces: Gabriella and Arianna, who at age 8 and 5 have an entire world of possibility ahead of them. They are living messengers to a world I will never see. May they discover the tenets of success early and live the life they want to lead. Always remembering how much their Tío Wilson loves them.

Finally to you the reader, thanks for taking the time to read my book and support me as I live my dreams every day.

.

CONTENTS

DEDICATION iii

CONTENTS v

PROLOGUE i

FORWARD iii

INTRODUCTION v

ONE Living the Dream 1

TWO A is for Attitude 11

THREE B is for Beliefs 25

FOUR C is for Commitment 35

FIVE The Final Word - SUCCESS!! 51

REFERENCES 59

ABOUT THE AUTHOR 62

PROLOGUE

Time stops for no one and this book reminds me of that. I wrote this book right after I completed my dissertation as a graduate student. I was in that ABD (all but dissertation) loop waiting to complete my doctorate. I was restless and used that energy to create a personal philosophy of success. Thus began my ABC Vision mantra. I did finish my PhD in 2002 and was the first Latino graduate with a doctorate from the Political Science program from Auburn University.

This book was originally published in 2003 with the title *Remember Your ABCs* and this is a new edition of the book. I have not made any substantial changes to the body of the work except for this prologue and the new title *ABC Vision*.

The world has changed tremendously since then. No one predicted that we would have smart phones, social media, or have broken the color barrier by electing our first African American President, Barrack Obama.

In many ways the world is a better place, full of opportunities. However we still have challenges. Most of these troubles are rooted within us. We are limited by the obstacles created in our minds. I hope that this book will be the key to unlock your full potential. I do not motivate, or claim to do so, only you can motivate yourself. But as an intellectual and man of ideas, I know that you can harness the power to be a success and live you're the life you want to lead!

Enjoy the book and start creating your dreams today, or if not, someone will hire you to build their's.

Dr. Wilson L. Triviño - @abcvision
ABC Vision Innovation Center
Atlanta, Georgia USA
August 14, 2015

Dr. Wilson L. Triviño @abcvision

FORWARD

By former Georgia U.S. Senator Max Cleland

Wilson Triviño has always been special. When I first met him, he was a young intern in the Georgia Legislature and I was serving as Georgia's Secretary of State, I knew then he would be a standout in whatever field he chose. He introduced himself as "Wilson like a 'tennis ball' and Triviño, like the 'golfer'." He knew how to make a lasting impression even as a young man.

His love for books, politics, and government has carried him to great achievements, and has allowed him to become the first Latino to earn a PhD in Political Science from Auburn University. Wilson has lived his book, which is what makes it so fascinating to read.

Through inspirational words and a number of activities, Wilson Triviño refreshes the insight that, although life is not always as easy as our ABCs, living life to the fullest is as simple as ABC: our Attitudes, Beliefs, and Commitment determine the course of our lives. Dr. Triviño not only challenges us to have the life we want to have, but he shows us how to do it.

This book is a great tool and a must read for anyone wanting a greater level of success and satisfactions in life.

INTRODUCTION

"It is never too late to be what you might have been."
-George Eliot

Way to go!! I want to congratulate you. You are now one step closer to accomplishing your dreams and living the life YOU want to lead!! Everything you have ever wanted can now come true. Take a moment and ask yourself these questions and answer them honestly:

- Are you happy?

- Do you have faith?

- Are your days filled with optimism and hope?

- Is every day full of new opportunities?

- Do you love yourself?

- Do you love others?

- Are you physically, emotionally, and spiritually balanced?

- Are you where you expected to be at in this stage of your life's journey?

- Do you love your job?

- Do you have financial security?

- Are you closer to your dreams today than you were yesterday?

Regardless of how we answer these questions, we all need to ask them to help us focus on what we want to accomplish in our life's journey. Each day we must face life's challenges, so why not become proactive instead of reactive? All of us have hopes and dreams, so why not live our dreams instead of imagining them? It seems ashame to allow your destiny to be controlled by self-created obstacles. Why not do something about it?

This exercise may seem very academic and you may be saying, "Yes, I have heard these words before." However, my question to you is: What are you going to do about it? Are you ready to move from being a spectator to become a participant? Are you willing to become a life experiencer? You decide!

Why did I write this book?

I wrote this book because I have always been interested in people and why they do the things that they do. Why do some people succeed and others fail? I believe that success generates lessons and these lessons can transcend various situations. My interest stems from this knowledge and my objective is to translate that information into a simple formula that anyone can use. Defining, creating, and living your success is the core theme of this book and my life's passion.

In my travels, I often see individuals who on the surface appear to have everything. They have wealth, fame, and access to all the pleasures of life, while others have nothing. Common sense would point to the person with all the good things in life as being the winner, while the one with nothing appears to be the loser.

Realistically, what commonly occurs is that the individual who has all the material benefits often merely exists, and does not actually live life to the fullest. They complain, are filled with a negative outlook, and do not see the possibilities in the world around them. They have settled into a rut and stopped growing. We all know people like this - are you one? At the same time, others may lack material wealth yet still be truly happy and rejoice every day in the simple pleasures of life.

This book is about helping you take the first step in the direction of your dreams. You are at a crossroad and as Yogi Berra said, "When you get to a fork in the road, take it!" The journey of a thousand miles begins with one step. Begin your journey with baby steps and accelerate until you are running toward your dreams.

I am not saying that success is just the ability to make lots of money, because if that were true everyone in the United States would be successful when compared to the rest of the world. My message to you is that you can reach your own level of success, which is defined as living the life YOU want to lead. This kind of success means much more than accumulating all the money, power, or fam the world has to offer. It is the key to unlocking inner peace, love, and happiness. We are the creators of our own universe.

Let me give you an example. A few years ago, I was at a point where life was not going my way. Quite simply, I was not happy. I felt that I was just existing and not living life to the fullest. Yes, I had the outer appearance of success, but I had lost the inner drive that made me jump out of bed in the morning and tackle life's opportunities. I was wandering aimlessly in the journey of life rather than taking charge and moving in the right direction. Then one day I decided to change the way I looked at life. I began to take a new approach, seeking solutions to problems and finding my way to where I wanted to be. The ABCs method resulted from this moment of self-discovery.

Over the years, I have met and learned from world-class thinkers and leaders. I have also read thousands of books, listened to countless speakers, and attended hundreds of seminars. They all share nuggets of wisdom, but what do they have in common? How can I combine these ideas into a message that anyone can immediately apply to their life in a way that can make a remarkable difference? I wrote *ABC Vision* to provide a roadmap that will empower you and remind you to focus on what is important to you every day.

Everyone has his or her own unique journey; in the path there are mountaintops and valleys. Not until you have reached the bottom of the lowest valley can you enjoy the view from the top of the highest mountain. Regardless of where you are today, you too can climb the highest peaks with a passion with every step. Come, join me and let us begin this journey today.

ONE Living the Dream

"The dreams of today are the realities of tomorrow."
-Franklin Delano Roosevelt

Every moment is a step into the unknown; today is a new day no matter how we perceive time. Time is more than the mere ticking away of the opportunity clock; it is a measure of continual change within the universe. Time is not linear or finite; it is constant motion. This instant can forever change your life.

Now take a moment and reflect on what defines you at this point in time: not as a person but as an artist. True artists create and express the universe within and around themselves. Ask yourself, what is my life's portrait? Your paints and brushstrokes are the choices you make each day. How do you feel about your portrait so far? Have you defined yourself as the person you always wanted to be or are you a "work in progress?" Are you reaching your limits as a human being by actively growing? Or, do you feel unfulfilled, lethargic, and numb when attempting to capture the meaning that you most desire in your life?

What is your mission in life and how is your purpose contributing to the universe? Does your philosophy of life serve as a guiding beacon, illuminating the path to wisdom and personal fulfillment? To help you with answering these questions, this chapter will explore problems, choices, and solutions.

Today we can find the best of times and the worst of times. No matter what state you are in at this moment, you have positive and negative energy around you. Consider how often we hear people say things like:

> Everything in my life is moving so quickly - I just can't seem to keep up. There are so many forces that are pushing and pulling me in different directions. Most of the time, I feel that I'm just reacting to situations, jumping from crisis to crisis, and not steering an independent course for myself. What choice do I have? I seem to spend a lot of time pretending to be someone I'm not. I lack confidence in my ideas, my perceptions, and myself. I'm worried people won't like the "real me", and so I try to present an image that I think they will respond to. Who is the "real me"? What values should govern my life? These are essential questions, but I just don't have time to think about what kind of person I want to be.

Can you relate to these reflective observations? These words capture so much of what individuals feel about the state of their lives in this 24/7, information-overloaded world. What is very interesting about these comments is that the Greek philosopher, Socrates, wrote them over 2,500 years ago. He posed these questions at a time when none of the modern conveniences and technologies existed that dominate our lives today. Can you imagine a world without telephones, the Internet, or CNN? Socrates wrote his comments in a time when much of the planet had yet to be explored. So how do these statements hold true today for you? He was talking about what we deal with every day of our lives today: the human experience.

I recently saw a great bumper sticker that stated, "SAVE THE HUMANS". How appropriate! We rarely take the time to re-energize and develop our human potential. Life's journey is uncharted and full of unexpected twists and turns. Our attention is scattered over a wide range of priorities, passing over the exploration and development of the human mind. You are the only person on this earth who can use your abilities.

Many individuals are far too busy "surviving" to wonder why they are living or who is doing the living. We so often cruise along on autopilot - days slipping into weeks, weeks merging into years, years fusing into a life - without confronting the basic question of who we are?

We all need to WAKE UP and take the leap into living our dream today!! As Zig Ziglar is fond of saying, "You can be what you want to be and you can go where you want to go! !" This idea is simple to preach, yet so hard to put into practice.

Problems: Why do we have them?

Years ago, I attended a lecture by Norman Vincent Peale and his ideas gave me a new insight into the human psyche. During this talk, he argued that everyone has problems. Problems do not discriminate based on race, wealth, or gender. Simply put, everyone has problems and the only people who do not have problems are those who are already "six feet under." Furthermore, if you don't have problems, you should get on your knees and pray that you find some, otherwise you are headed to the only place where people can rest in peace: the local cemetery.

People come and go, but problems are here to stay. Don't fret about your problems; rejoice in them because it means that you are ALIVE. No matter who or what caused your problems, only you can solve them! That's it! We are constantly bombarded with great opportunities brilliantly disguised as insoluble problems. This book will give you the tools to deal with life's daily challenges and help you to find a vision of your own success.

Choices: Where do we start?

The best way to start is to DECIDE to start. This word is so simple, but yet so powerful. In my travels across the country many tell me "But, I just can't." I respond, "Why not?" They list every possible excuse. Regroup, get on track, and get started! The first step toward overcoming your problems is to stop focusing on the problem and instead focus on the solution. As Dale Carnegie stresses, "**W**orry **O**nly **R**educes the **R**esources within **Y**ou! (**WORRY**)."

Before you can go any further, you need to let go of the past. No matter what happened last year, yesterday, this morning, or three seconds ago, it is in the past. You have to acknowledge that the past does not equal the future. Yes, let me repeat it again, THE PAST DOES NOT EQUAL THE FUTURE.

If I were to say to you: "I am going to give you $86,400 to spend today," what would you spend it on? The only catch is that you cannot give it away or invest it in anything. You have to spend it all today. Could you do it? Would you do it? How would you do it? Pause for a moment and consider this. What would you do with all that money? What if I said you already do just that? Every day you spend that amount -- not in dollars but in time. The figure 86,400 represents the amount of seconds found within each twenty-four hour period. Many of us fritter it away watching television, worrying, or simply doing nothing, yet once it is gone, it is gone. We all have a limited amount of time. Life is simply a series of passages and this poem reminds us of the importance of time every day:

> Our life is but a grain of sand in the oceans,
> And but a second in time.
> Don't get caught up in working for the Future that you forget to live today.
> Take the time to notice and enjoy the Small things of today, because eventually,
> Today will become tomorrow and will Be remembered as yesterday.
>   -Anonymous

Before I go any further, take a minute to do this simple exercise:
Go to a quiet place outside or inside and put this book aside for a minute. In this minute, close your eyes, listen, and observe what you feel. Go on – try it.

Welcome back; what did you feel? Most individuals whom I ask to do this exercise say different things they feel their bodily functions such as their breathing, their heart pumping, and their blood flowing. The more perceptive individuals describe a presence of someone or something around them. That presence is your spirit. This spirit is what makes you and me and everyone else unique. We can be in a room full of people, yet deep inside we are all alone.

The spirit we fell is awareness. This is the one constant force through our lives. The ever present witnessing awareness. This ever present witnessing awareness was once a baby, once a teenager, now as an adult it is a part of your daily existence. Deepak Chopra leads these talks into consciousness and states "that everything comes and goes, the awareness stays, we need to learn to let go." Like holding your breath, you will choke, you need to learn to let go and realize that everything comes and goes. We are the ones who know ourselves best. Each of you has three personas: the public individual whom everyone sees, the loving individual whom your family sees, and the private individual whom no one sees but yourself.

Regardless of who or what you believe in, we are all spiritual beings. Most people feel that they are human beings with souls, when the opposite is closer to the truth. We are spiritual beings in a human form whose souls yearn to sing and soar to greatness. In our minds, we project and create the person that we are. Have you ever been stressed, angry, or burned-out and taken a vacation or a break from your routine? What happened? Did you all of a sudden feel better. If so, you changed your mental state. Change your focus and you will discover a new universe of possibilities instead of limitations. If you see it, you can achieve it!

By reflecting and realizing that you are a part of the larger universe, you will be able to acknowledge your uniqueness. In the entire history of the universe, the planet, and the human race, there has never existed a person exactly like you. There are seven billion individuals on Earth and no two are exactly alike. Even twins who are genetically identical carry different personalities and thoughts.

If you are willing to accept this premise, you will never feel alone. How so, you might ask? Think about it. All living creatures exist in the world within the universe. Everything is synchronized and moves to the same rhythm. This balance connects all living creatures together and enables the fragile cycle of life to exist. If you do not believe this fact, go outside and observe the world around you. Simply experience life- the birds, see the trees, and see the tiny ants, all existing and working in perfect harmony.

In order to be able to define your own happiness, you need to focus on identifying what is making you unhappy. The most obvious obstacle to finding inner peace is dealing with and solving the problems we face after deciding to become proactive instead of reactive to the world around us.

Solutions: A Road Map to Success

Unfortunately, because of the fast-paced world we live in, we allow our environment to control us rather than taking control of our environment. The title, *ABC Vision,* represents three constant forces that will empower you to shape your destiny. They are represented by the letters **A**, **B**, and **C** that stand for:

A - Attitude
B - Beliefs
C - Commitment

So what is this book, ABCs, all about? I came up with the title of this book from observing children. When you see young children in grade school, regardless of race, color, or gender, you see them full of hope and optimism. They have a core sense of self and do not get caught up with the limitations imposed by society. They are excited about life, eager to learn, and are not afraid to challenge conventional wisdom. Together, they play and explore their world with a sense of excitement. Like sponges, they soak up ideas and live life. Ask them what they want to do when they are grownups and they will give you a list of exciting occupations, such as astronauts, firemen, and doctors.

Now fast-forward to what is commonly found with adults. Have you ever gone to a place and seen the people act like zombies; a place filled with lack of enthusiasm, hope, and optimism? It is as though the spirit has been drained out of them. They just exist and don't live! I have known people who can't get out of bed because they hate what they do and feel trapped in their bleak world. How can we have forgotten what we took for granted in childhood?

The following chapters will expand on the value of your Attitude, Beliefs, and Commitment. This simple device will become a technique that will allow you to tackle life's journey and, by becoming aware of these ideas, empower you to live your dreams. Remember that long ago when you learned your ABCs, it didn't stop there. You put them together to make words and then sentences that conveyed ideas. Similarly, the ideas found within this book will help you begin the process of moving toward living the life that you want to lead.

Life is not a destination but a journey filled with experiences and lessons. The purpose of life is a life of purpose. My purpose and what makes me happy is to help others. That is why I am called to public service and to speak to audiences across the country. I believe that service is the price you pay for living.

This book is not a cure-all, but I know it will serve as a catalyst in awakening the giant from within and empower you to become a "no limit" person. Be proud that you are finally taking a bold step toward being able have *ABC Vision*. Let's begin!

TWO A is for Attitude

"The meaning of things lies not in the things themselves but in our attitude toward them."
-Antoine de Saint Eupery

Attitude = Vision Where do you want to go?

Attitude is really the most important component of becoming successful. Your attitude is the mental outlook that shapes your perception of reality. You choose what you become. Destiny is achieved either consciously or unconsciously, and you determine your fate. By being conscious of your attitude, you can become more open to new possibilities. The person you are today is a result of all the decisions you have made up to this point in your life. Whatever the mind of an individual can conceive, they can achieve. You alone bear the responsibility of shaping your own destiny.

As Robert Schuller has written:

> The longer I live, the more I realize the impact of attitude on life. Attitude, to me, is more important than facts, it is more important than the past, than education, than money, than success, than what other people say, think, or do. It is more important than appearance, giftedness or skill. It will make or break a company, a church, or a home. The remarkable thing about life is that we have

choices and decisions to make every day. We cannot change our past; we cannot change the inevitable. The only thing we can do is play on the one string we have, and that is our attitude. I am convinced that life is 10% what happens to me and 90% of how I react to it. And so it is with you, we can charge of our attitudes.

This is so eloquently expressed and so true; you are the only one who can determine your attitude. Realize that you were born with the seeds of potential greatness.

Once while sitting in Dr. Schuller's Chyrstal Cathedral in Garden Groove, California, I was in awe with the glorious blue California sky. My spirit was connected with the heavens. On that beautiful day, Dr. Schuller asked each of us, to take a deep breathe.

I now ask you to do it. Go on take a deep breathe. Hold on to it, then a big exhale. What do you feel? A sense of release? Well that is the feeling of hope, according to Dr. Schuller. We all have hope within us and that is how you can take on change and ride its wave into possibility.

What determines the path your life will take is your reaction to life's experiences. Your attitude influences how you interact with the world around you, either positively or negatively. Each day is a series of decisions about life's journey. What shall I wear? What will I do? What will I experience? The decision-making process is a complex one involving choices influenced by our past experiences and desires. A clear and positive mental attitude enables us to think from the perspective of possibility rather than seeing only the limitations.

We have two futures in front of us: the one that we drift into or the one that we choose. Why not you go after the future you want and live your dreams? At this point you might be saying, "Okay, I acknowledge that attitude is an important component of success, but what do I need to do to get into the habit of having a good attitude?" We will now move on to the steps you can take to discover how to develop your own positive attitude. This chapter will look into some important components of a healthy attitude and how you can shape it. The steps toward shaping your mental attitude are: acceptance, assessment, and action.

Acceptance

The first step in developing a good attitude is acceptance. Be honest, face the truth and take responsibility for your life! One major problem in the American culture is that we blame others when we need to take responsibility for ourselves. "It's the government's fault," "it's our parents' fault," "the Internet is to blame," "the Devil made me do it," and on and on. These excuses are total nonsense; all the decisions that we have made in the past have led us to this point in time. The most vivid example of this is our health. The food we ate, the exercise we did or did not do, and the amount of care we have taken of the body that houses our spirit. Our bodies are temples and we should worship and care for them like a shrine. We should also care for our mental health. Our thoughts, dreams, and interactions with other people all influence our mental attitude. Our minds create the world around us and, like a parachute, will only function when open.

Life is a series of pictures we focus on and then process. Think about it: when you are taking pictures, do you capture everything? No, you only ever manage to include a small portion of the vast and complex panorama in front of you. This was brought home to me forcibly when I traveled to the interior of Alaska and was awestruck by all the beauty of nature. The photographs I took could not begin to do justice to nature's miracle. If you really want to experience the last American frontier, go to Alaska. There you will see what it was like for the early settlers of the wilderness: the mountains, trees, and nature existing in harmony and at peace. There is no way I can describe everything I experienced: the stillness and cold of the air, the quiet of the night, the noises of nature, and the magic of the aurora lighting up the night-time sky. This led to me think that attitude can be compared to a photograph; you have to compose your picture carefully, focusing on what is good and leaving out what is bad. Everyone has a photographic memory, but some just don't have film in their camera.

Everything that happens to us can be traced back to the actions we have taken throughout our lives. If you are not satisfied with where you are in life, change it. It is as simple as that. But first, you must reach a level of acceptance that you have created the life you live today. Don't blame others, take responsibility and let go of the past.

Our bodies are a physical manifestation of our daily decisions. What we consume, what we wear, and what we project to the world around us. As in our physical representation, our consciousness reflects what we feed our mind and spirit.

You might ask, "Well, how can I transform my current attitude into a winning attitude?" The simplest approach to improving one's attitude is to always be positive. Think success, not failure. One of my favorite quotes is from Gene Kranz, the flight director for the Apollo 13 mission, whose astronauts were marooned in space, unable to return to Earth. Instead of panicking and giving up hope, Kranz responded to this perilous situation by declaring: "Failure is not an option." What an unbelievable statement! Can you imagine if everything you attempted was with this mental focus? It would create a new world of opportunity. Imagine a world in which you could not fail. What would you attempt? What would you do differently than what you are doing right now in your life?

The next thing to realize is that, as simple as it sounds, you create your own reality. Yes, you actually do create your own reality. Our reality is a result of our mental focus and perception. Conduct this exercise with a friend. Take a moment, look around the room, and ask him or her to focus on all the things that are red. Have them close their eyes for 30 seconds. After 15 seconds, ask them to list everything that is blue. Write down their responses, and after they open their eyes compare the list with the blue items around them. Did they miss a few things? They probably did not notice many blue things, even those that were very obvious, because they were focusing on the red objects. Lesson: focus on the positive things around you. This can become very habit forming; Zig Ziglar who is so positive used to say he had a friend that he does not develop film "because of all the negatives."

I attended a speech given by Dr. Deepak Chopra and he gave a great example. He suggested that our minds work like living television sets. We experience the projection on the screen but it's something that we create in our own mind. Crack open the screen and you will find a box filled with wires and circuits; you won't find Larry King, beautiful beaches, or the magic of television. Another example: how do we recognize the colors around us? By a series of actions, our brain transforms the light that enters our eyes into an interpretation of the world we see around us. Everything we see and experience is our perception of reality; we create the world in which we live. In other words, no one decides for us whether we can have a good day or a bad day. We are the ones who make this decision.

Dale Carnegie says, "Think enthusiasm and you will become enthusiastic." Some may criticize this as being too simplistic, arguing that being positive is not a cure-all and I agree that being positive will not always solve everything. This may surprise you. I can almost hear you exclaiming, "What! Being positive is not a cure-all? That can't be!" Yes, it's true that positive thinking alone can't help you. You need to be proactive. For instance, if you care for your garden and find that it *is* full of weeds, what do you do? You can say, "There are no weeds, there are no weeds, there are no weeds." What will happen to your garden? The weeds will overtake it! How do you prevent this? You pull the weeds and let the garden grow and produce. Weeds (negative thoughts) are everywhere, but by taking the time to pull them out by the roots, they will be permanently removed from your garden. Learn to cultivate your garden and remember life's dearest lesson- knowing when to hang on and learning when to let go. As Ralph Waldo Emerson was fond of saying:

> Enthusiasm is one of the most powerful engines of success. When you do a thing, do it with all your might. Put your whole soul into it. Stamp it with your own personality. Be active, be energetic, be enthusiastic and faithful and you will accomplish your objective. Nothing great was ever achieved without enthusiasm!"

You have to feed your mind; like a sponge, it will absorb new ideas and, like a sponge, it will release the good or bad that you put into it. As Winston Churchill expressed, "Personally, I'm always ready to learn, although I do not always like being taught." Be ready to learn.

Robert Schuller warned that everybody needs to be continually evolving and changing their attitudes. You need to make the leap from being a positive thinker into becoming a power thinker. Positive thinking is mere faith and possibility thinking is faith that is focused, but power thinking is focused faith filled with the power to follow through.

Faith + Focus + Follow = Through SUCCESS

Your attitude will help you realize that today's accomplishments were yesterday's impossibilities.

Why not simply press on? Obstacles are seldom the same size tomorrow as they are today. Take action! This can be so simple yet so hard. Be willing to attempt to move forward. Be willing to be a risk taker instead of a risk avoider.

Dale Carnegie's formula is a great way to cultivate a mental attitude that will bring you peace and happiness. You need to fill your mind with thoughts of peace, courage, health and hope. Never try to get even with your enemies, as it's only wasted effort. Expect ingratitude. Every day count your blessings - not your troubles. Do not imitate others, be yourself and listen to your inner voice. Finally, and best of all, create happiness for others. If all else fails, the best way to overcome any obstacle is to pray.

Assessment

Einstein once said, "The solution to a problem will never come from the same level of understanding that created the problem in the first place." I believe that what he meant is that we need to take a step back from the problem in order to see the solution. Stepping back is another way of saying "stop focusing on the problem and find a solution."

Initially, all you need to get in the right frame of mind is to explore what holds you back from controlling your attitude. Sit down, relax, and do these exercises. First you need to make a gratitude list. Negative experiences tend to distort the world around you, but a little reflection on what has been wonderful about this day, week, or year will put things back into perspective.

After you complete this list, you will have something to turn to for inspiration no matter how bad things seem. Keep in mind that there are far more good things in life than bad. In reviewing your gratitude list, focus your energy on something you enjoy and have total control over. For me, this means cooking, writing, or visiting with a good friend. The more I indulge in hobbies, the better my attitude gets. The third and most effective attitude adjuster is to make someone else happy - this works miracles. This is tough when you are feeling down, but after you do it you will feel like a winner. I enjoy doing random acts of kindness like giving flowers to a stranger, paying the toll for the driver behind me, or picking up the phone and talking to a friend. All these work wonders. Think out loud - Who can you make really happy today?

List Them HERE:

Gratitude List:

Things over which I have total control:

Actions that will make someone else happy:

Now that you can see on the page all the good things in your life, take a hard look and ask yourself, "Where am I at this stage in my life?" Examine your physical, intellectual, emotional, and spiritual roles and how you stand. Are you totally satisfied? Be honest and remember, once you have taken responsibility, you can free yourself up to do something about it. List them now:

Physical:

Intellectual:

Emotional:

Spiritual:

You have to know what you want your outcome to be before you will ever be able to achieve it. This does not mean that the road to success will be easy, but good judgment guarantees success. Remember though, that good judgment is the product of experience, and experience is the product of poor judgment. Simple lesson; you have to be part of the game in order to win.

Action

The philosopher Aristotle once said, "For the things we have to learn before we can do them, we learn by doing them." The crucial step in controlling your attitude is by taking action. Goals are nothing without action. Don't be afraid to get started now. Just do it.

As I said earlier when I was explaining why I wrote this book, children have an amazing way of being dreamers. It doesn't matter if you've had children in your life - only that you've been one. Ask a child what he wants to do and he will tell you: astronaut, actress, doctor, or other wonderful careers. Now go and ask a person working for a large bureaucratic organization. What do you want to do? Did you start out in your career wanting to be a mid-level supervisor? Or did you just want to be a paper pusher? How about a brown-noser?

I love that commercial with the children who solemnly stare into the camera and say, "I want to be stuck in a dead end job working in a small cubicle." The commercial highlights how most adults drift into their current position instead of plunging into the magic of their dreams. Break the cycle. Live your dreams; better yet, write down all the things you want to do in your life. Take 20 minutes to do so and act as if no matter what you want to do you cannot fail. By writing this list, it will do two things: it will help you focus and visualize your dream and it will allow you to say to yourself, "Hey, that can be done." Don't limit yourself: be wild. For example, you might write down, "I want to travel in the space shuttle." Most people say that is nuts! But don't tell that to Dennis Vito, a Californian. He was an average businessman who found a way to be the world's first tourist in space. This would never have happened if he had not reached out and created an opportunity that allowed him to fulfill his dreams by paying the Russian government to take him for the ride of a lifetime. What an awesome feat!

At this moment, list all the things that you want to do in your life: We forget how limited our time is on Earth. Picture yourself as a ninety year-old person and look back over your life's journey. Did you do everything you wanted? If not, now you have a chance to redirect your life. In your dreams, there are no limitations. You can fly, travel through time, occupy different bodies and transcend the physical limitations created by rational thought. From this state, you can open yourself up to a world of new possibilities. Just for fun, write the things that you really want to do with your life. Don't hold back: dare to dream!

What do I want to do with my life?

What would you do if I told you that I could give you the key to unlock the secret of achieving your dreams? This information would be priceless; it would be worth more than all the money in the world. Well then, why don't you seek this key? I know that success leaves clues and these clues empower us to get closer to our dreams.

Look around you and connect with people who have overcome obstacles and live a successful life every day. More importantly, learn from them.

In every city, there is a public library full of books about individuals who changed human history. These people all saw the same sunrise and sunset that we see; they breathed the same air and drank the same water. They experienced life as we do. What made them different from us is that they achieved greatness and we didn't. So, why don't we learn from them?

Don't reinvent the wheel; use your energy to create new ideas. As Harry Truman said, "Not all readers are leaders, but all leaders are readers." Find the patterns of success; use the technique of modeling, which is to model the actions of what successful people have done to create the life that you want. It is easier to study history than to begin from scratch. Knowing where you have been is so important because it helps you to get where you want to go more easily. Life is a challenge, so try it!

Another important way to improve your attitude and reach your dream is to build alliances. This is more than mere networking, as it is actually building and developing relationships with these winning people. Get a mentor. My life has been enriched because I have filled it with people who have a stake my success. They have helped me to develop as a person and to experience things that have empowered me and allowed me to get closer to my dreams. However, I had to be open enough to ask for help and listen to the responses. You will be amazed at how accessible these people will be and how willing they are to share their story. There are no such things as strangers, just friends you have not yet met.

You need to network with winners. In every community, there are people who are the leaders. They can be the town elders, elected representatives, entrepreneurs, civic activists, academics or any other responsible citizen. These people did not all start at this point, but began like everyone else, at the bottom.

So why not build relationships with them and learn from their life experience?

Not only will you learn from them, but they will also have networks of their own, which can only add to your circle of influence. In the best book on networking, *Dig Your Well Before You are Thirsty,* Harvey Mackey writes, "No matter how smart you are, no matter how talented, you can't do it alone." Think about what you want and spend a lifetime getting it, one piece at a time. And remember that this is a two-way street: as Zig Ziglar likes to point out, "You can get what you want as long as you help other people get what they want."

Taking baby steps will get you closer to your dreams, but doing nothing will get you nowhere. What do you have to lose? Just try it! By having the right attitude, there is nothing you cannot do. History is full of individuals who walked the talk and lived their dreams.

In a commencement speech, television commentator Chris Matthews shared his "secret of success." He began with several simple steps: get a seat at the table of your chosen game, don't be afraid to ask for help, and do something you love. What wise words! Don't be afraid; begin today. Put 110% of your efforts into living your dreams. Hard work never hurt anyone. Guess what, your success will become more meaningful if your work becomes your play. Enjoy life to the fullest; play hard and work hard.

The time to plan for the next twenty years is right now, not twenty years from now. In the next chapter you will learn about the foundation of our existence, our beliefs.

THREE B is for Beliefs

'The future belongs to those who believe in the beauty of their dreams."
-Eleanor Roosevelt

Beliefs = Core Values = Why do I want to do this?

Regardless of whether you are conscious of it or not, you make all the decisions in your life based upon your beliefs. Your beliefs are the congruent internal representation that governs your behavior. They are formed as a result of the sum of your experiences throughout your life so far and have created the foundation on which you stand, determining what you can or can't do. This chapter will enable you to re-examine your beliefs and become conscious of how they guide you each day in this chapter, you need to first break free from the past and understand the limitations it creates. Begin the process and believe in challenging yourself and answering the right questions. Then consciously you will discover the awesome potential that lies within you.

Break free from the Past

Rejoice, for today is a new day!! Happiness is a readjusted mental attitude. As Victor Franki wrote, "Man's search for meaning is the primary motivation in his life. This meaning is unique and specific in that it must and can be fulfilled by him alone; only then does it achieve a significance which will satisfy his own will to meaning."

Each individual is responsible for what happens to them in the future, regardless of what has happened in the past. Think about this. No matter what happened yesterday, last year or decades ago, it is gone. Time moves forward. The past is gone and the future has not yet arrived, so all we can control is the present. We have to learn to live in the present! You have to realize that no one can go back and make a brand new start. However, anyone can start from now and make a brand new ending. One of our greatest illusions is that there will be more time tomorrow to do the things we need to do today.

Before you are able to move toward your dreams, you need to cleanse your mind of the negative experiences and forces that prevent you from reaching these dreams. These limitations are found within the confines of your mind. By freeing yourself from the past, you will be empowered. It will transform you into a new person: a fresh new soul that has been released from the prison of yesterday's limitations. Yesterday is experience. Tomorrow is hope. Today is getting from one moment to another as best we can.

You might ask, "How do I do this?" Pause for a moment and reflect on some negative experiences that have prevented you from tackling new challenges such as a personal failure, an inconsiderate comment, or a bad experience. Taken into account, all these can add up to a very powerful reason why you are not taking action now on what you know is possible.

Take a moment and write down ten negative events that have happened to you in your life. Some of you might say, "I could write a whole book of my failures," but on the next page list the ten negative experiences you most vividly remember and the reasons that they create worry in your life. For instance, you might say "the other kids laughed at me in school, I did not feel smart enough, and I felt inadequate." Complete this list honestly.

Your list of hard-hitting life altering events

1.
2.
3.
4.
5.
6.
7.
8.
9.
10.

Now that you have listed ten things that are giving you a headache, look at discovering your inner self. Ask yourself, how do these events prevent me from accomplishing what I want to do? Why do I allow the past to determine my future? Who is responsible for my current situation? The answer is simple - YOU! Realize that something is going to happen, it's up to you! What separates the winners from the losers is that the losers see negative experiences as failure, while the winners see them as temporary roadblocks and find a detour around them.

No matter what has caused your problems, only you can solve them. You create your own reality and this reality is something that results from your years of conditioning. By taking responsibility and freeing yourself from guilt, you are able to move forward. Right
now, take out a sheet of paper and write down everything that negatively influences your attitude and then relate the list to the decisions you have made about these items. Review this list and your problems and ask yourself why they are taking so much of your precious time. Ask yourself these questions about every problem you are facing.

- What is the problem?

- What are some of the causes of the problem?

- What are some viable solutions?

- Which approaches am I going to use today in order to get closer to a final result?

Use the answers to analyze the situation and seek a path toward resolution.

Beliefs

Modern psychological research has concluded that the focus determines the outcome. Think about the National Aeronautical and Space Agency's (NASA) focus during its push to put a man on the moon after President John F. Kennedy set the target of accomplishing it by the end of the decade.

Everyone at NASA was pumped and ready to do it! Someone asked a janitor who worked at NASA what he did there. Instead of saying that he was cleaning floors or toilets, he replied, "I am helping put a man on the moon!" WOW!! How clear can you get? That is a powerful statement; he felt he was an integral part of the goal! How does this translate to one's personal life? Think of the power of knowing where you are going and, better yet, why?

Although psychologists usually agree on very little, they do agree that the strongest force on earth is one's need to be in perceived control of one's universe. This can only happen with constant self-analysis and focus on identifying our beliefs. By acknowledging your beliefs, you will be able to discover how you can use them in your daily actions.

How do you discover your personal philosophy? First, begin with how you view yourself. Answer this question:

I am _____.

What word or words did you use to fill in the blank? Was it your profession, your status, your role in your family? We each have within us a picture of who and what we are. Regardless of how we answer, this projection of ourselves to the world has an impact on how society treats us. Do we hide behind labels or do we truly feel comfortable in our own skin. Now answer the more important question, "What is the meaning of my life?"

Deepak Chopra says that "Our bodies are a physical print out of the collective decisions of our lives." Think about this for a minute. Look at yourself in the mirror in the morning before you get dressed. By seeing yourself with nothing on but a smile, it will help you see the physical core that makes up you. Your weight, the way you carry yourself, the number of wrinkles you have are all outward physical signs of decisions you have made. The stress you create in your life, the food you have eaten, the jokes you have laughed at are all part of your past decisions.

Believe it or not, you have been working on your philosophy of life for a long time. It is the core of your being. A brilliant analogy used by Stephen Covey is that of a compass. When using a compass, true north is always the same regardless of where you may be on the planet. Your beliefs should serve as your true North. It defines what is right and wrong and where you should focus your energies. A philosophy is more than simply a collection of random thoughts; it is what sets the direction of your daily actions.

We already constantly analyze situations, whether we are
conscious of it or not. Every decision we make is an attempt to maximize pleasure and reduce pain. We do things because we think they will make us feel better. Why are you reading this book? Hopefully you are reading it because you want to gain the knowledge that will give you the ability to achieve the pleasure of your dreams.

Your beliefs are best defined as the congruent internal representation that governs behavior. What creates beliefs? Five specific factors define your belief system. They are your environment, events in your life, knowledge, past results, and goals. If you live in poverty maybe are likely in despair and feel like the world lacks hope. If you grew up in an environment like the one I had, with entrepreneurial parents and positive support, then you believe in opportunity over adversity. The events in your life also shape your view. If you have witnessed success, you will be more likely to reach for success. Knowledge is also an important key to a winning belief system. An education makes you realize that the more you learn the less you know and opens your mind's eye to a world of possibility. That is why continuous learning is a must for continuous success. Past results determine your fate; if you have been successful throughout your life you will feel that you can reach for success. If you have always deemed your actions a failure, then you will fail in your actions. Finally, and probably the most important factor in your belief system is to be self-aware. Why do you do the things you do? Reflect and look inward. If you have a vision and know what you want from life, you will reach beyond your grasp and push yourself to the outer limits. Seek and you shall receive.

Beliefs serve as our core values. By being able to specifically identify core beliefs, we are better able to feel that we are a part of the larger universe and know what our life's purpose is. That is why a personal mission statement is the key to creating the life you want to lead. What is the purpose of your life, why do you do the things you do?

Begin

The biggest obstacle facing any new challenge is to sit down and begin. So we begin anew. One step can make a difference!! Charles Gould wrote a poem that is one of my favorites and describes how a single step can move you in the direction of your dreams:

One song can spark a memory
One flower can waken a dream,
One tree can start a forest,
One bird can herald spring,
One smile can start a friendship,
One handclasp can lift a soul,
One star can guide a ship at sea,
One speech can set a goal.
One vote can change a nation,
One sunbeam can light a room.
One candle can erase the darkness,
One laugh can chase the gloom.
One step must start, each journey,
One word must start each prayer.
One hope can raise the spirits,
One prayer can show you care.
One can make a difference.
YOU CAN!

Right now you are going to create your mission statement. Don't worry about the term "mission statement" is a term often used for a statement that describes the shape of your life, for "taking stock of you." If you sit down and take time to reflect, you will remember that all of us have core values and beliefs that shape and determine our destiny. This foundation is what we build upon. For example, you could look at a hole in the ground and determine the dimensions of a building. How is your foundation? Begin to build the structure that will help you reach your dreams on a solid foundation.

Why are mission statements so important, you might ask? Mission statements make you clarify your beliefs. Do not limit yourself, but borrow ideas from the winning masters; how have others reached where you want to go? These forces enable you to move forward and create the compelling future that makes you "you." As the famed artist Edgar Degas explained, "It is all very well to copy what you see, but it is better to draw what you see in your mind ... then your memory and your imagination are freed from the tyranny imposed by nature."

The ability to accomplish your life's dreams is the ability to
focus. Ask yourself these questions:

> What are my beliefs; what do I stand for?
> What is my vision of the future?
> What do I want to accomplish?
> What is my creed, value, or life's philosophy?

> Take a moment and develop this into your personal mission statement.

> My mission statement is:

The words in this chapter speak volumes regarding the need to define yourself. Take your mission statement and memorize it; it should be your mantra and remind you of what you stand for every day in a positive way.

To look is one thing. To see what you are looking at is another. To understand what you see is a third. To learn from what you understand is still something else. But to act on what you learn is all that really matters.

Realize that there is only one you and there will only ever be one you. Be bold and beautiful! That uniqueness is what makes the impossible possible. Truly dream the impossible dream. Go on, try it! The next chapter will enable you to commit to your dreams and develop the courage to fight for them.

FOUR C is for Commitment

"If you have no idea where you are going, how will you know when you get there?"
-As Alice in Alice in Wonderland was told.

Commitment = focus =How will I get there?

Up to this point in the book, you have learned why you need to have a good attitude and to be aware of your beliefs. The next phase is to develop the commitment to stay the course. Life is a marathon, not a sprint. You have to stick it out through the bad times as well as the good. No one said living your dreams was going to be easy. It is tough to do but so are you. According to Robert Schuller, "Tough times never last but tough people do." Believe in yourself by maintaining your commitment. This will help you to focus and enable you to determine how you will achieve your goal. With the flexibility to weather the continual changes you will encounter in your life, a clear vision of where you are going, and the ability to continue your journey in spite of the obstacles that appear to block your path, commitment will surely become a part of your psyche. If you have a goal make it happen! Condition yourself to believe that failure is not an option.

Dr. Wilson L. Triviño @abcvision

Continual Change

I think the reason why people often lack the momentum to do something is their resistance to change. An old saying goes, "The only person who likes change is a wet baby." I am here to tell you that CHANGE is the only constant force in the universe. No matter what has happened to you in the past, the time to act is now. The past does not equal the future! The past is gone and the future is uncertain; the only thing we have the power to control is right now, this second, this moment of time. Life is full of changes: the seasons, the circle of life, and the passage of time. Nothing lasts forever and everything evolves into something else.

I always amazed by the tale of the dinosaur. These creatures were enormous, seemingly larger than life. They towered over all other living beings and ruled the Earth for thousands of years. But why are there no dinosaurs on the planet today? Many explanations have been suggested: shifts in the climate or the environment, a severe meteorite shower, or simple extinction. All these are valid explanations, but the bottom line is that they failed to adapt. They failed to change with the shifting conditions and this prevented them from being around today. Dinosaurs are extinct. The only dinosaurs that exist today are the skeletal remains on display in museums. Do you want to be in a museum, collecting dust and being gawked at by tourists? Smile for the camera - click. No way, you want to be part of the world and live!! Lesson learned: change before you have to. You can tackle change or quit!

In my research, have found that three factors accelerate change in our lives and have played major roles in producing the complex world that we live in today. These factors are the global economic revolution, the technological revolution, and the information revolution. There are over seven billion individuals now living on our planet, seeking to provide economic security for themselves and their families. We make up a diverse group, but we are all competing for the limited resources available on a single, aging planet.

The first of the factors that is accelerating change, the global economic revolution, has changed the way in which we relate to each other. We no longer worry about competing within our own communities or countries but against the more complex world economic markets. As Robert Reich explains in his book, *Success at Work*, the average American couple is working eleven more weeks than they did ten years ago. Chasing economic security is the norm, as the most successful workers seize any new opportunity that comes their way, "making hay while the sun shines."

The second cause of this increased rate of change is the technological revolution. The industrial age that led to the technological age was supposed to create a world in which we would have more leisure time. We were going to have robots to perform mundane tasks, reducing the work week and allowing us to enjoy more of life's simple pleasures. This has not occurred; the average individual is dependent on his computer, cell phone, and electronic gizmos to get through his day. The faster pace of life made possible by the widespread use of technology has shortened response times and increased efficiency. The objective is to bring costs down and produce widgets both more cheaply and faster than was possible even ten years ago.

The third factor driving the rapid changes we are experiencing in our lives is the information age, which has led to a global community. The Internet has done more than create a new economy; it has created a collective psyche. We can now belong to a world community without ever having to step over our doorstep. Enter any Internet chat café and you will see people sipping coffee and chatting with others from around the world, instead of with each other.

Our common experiences now revolve around what is seen on CNN, Fox News, or the Drudge Report. We mourn for complete strangers, like Princess Diana, racecar driver Dale Earnhart, or the crew of the space shuttle Challenger, but don't know our neighbors or the personal problems of the person sitting in the cubicle next to us. In spite of the tragic loss of human life, September 11, 2001 brought us together as a world civilization. The live television coverage of the events allowed people around the globe to experience the horror as it occurred. However, we also witnessed countless acts of kindness and heroism performed by regular people, just like you or me, who stepped forward to help others when it mattered most, often at the risk of their own lives. They reached deep within themselves and found the strength to do what had to be done. They were an inspiration to us all.

These events showed us as a society how fragile our system has become. The terrorist attacks disrupted global transportation, commerce, and communications networks. Yes, we recovered from the barbaric act, but we aware of our interdependency. People from many nations died that day in New York, Washington and Pennsylvania, and the shared global mourning united us as human beings. We are one people, regardless of where we happen to live on the planet.

One of the most moving speeches I have ever heard was made by former New York City Mayor, Rudy Giuliani. As he shared his experience of 9-11 and described seeing the sheer horror of that day's events, he also expressed his thoughts on facing death. "After the first tower fell, I was trapped and had to face my own mortality. Fortunately, with the help of others, I escaped." As he cheated death, he felt a responsibility to share this horror with the world and try to root out the evil that caused it. His life, was as most peoples, was changed forever by 9-11. As I spoke with him after the speech, I felt a connection to that day's historic events and shared his anguish. We are all mortals, and 9-11 dramatically showed the uncertainty of the future. Who would have thought that something so horrendous could happen in today's world.

The information revolution allowed the events of September 11 to be experienced simultaneously all over the world. "We are entering an era of no limits," writes Jeffrey Young in *Cisco Unauthorized*, "with nothing to break the cascade of human intelligence unleashed by the Information Age. The Web essentially allows all the brains on earth to communicate and share insights in real time, around the globe, all the time." "The network," writes

U.C. Berkeley professor, Manuel Castellas, "becomes the social structure of everything."

Information has also created information overload, where huge amounts of information and misinformation are jumbled together and it is next to impossible to make sense of the results. This was seen during the Clinton impeachment scandal, when most people knew all the intimate details of the Monica saga regardless of whether they were true or not.

But the cynics say that the Internet is just hype. The pundits on the financial channels can talk up a stock and create hype where hype has no reason to exist. Look at the destruction of the new economy with the falling number of stocks and the largest devaluation in early 2001. I say it is a blip on the screen. We are going through a tremendous transformation and this transformation is leading to a world we could not even imagine yesterday. What the market drop of 2001 tells us is that the Internet is not going away, but flawed business models are. In a speech to Georgia Tech graduate students, Jack Welch, the former chairman of General Electric, brought up a good point: "It's not that there is a new economy, but that it is the old economy principles employed in a better way." Imagine this: 100 years ago a man sat in his buggy selling oranges. His goal was to sell them at a price that would give him a profit, and put the oranges in the hands of someone who wanted to eat them. Today, the principle is the same: produce X, sell it to Y, and make Z profit. So if your business plan was no good in the old economy, it won't work in the new economy either. We have to move from "feel good" slogans and get down to the basics.

These forces are not altogether negative; they have led to a period of human existence where more people have access to opportunity. I am always reminded that the richest monarch or individual one hundred years ago did not have access to one percent of what we have today. We can communicate with people on the other side of the planet, jump on an airplane and fly between continents, and have access to financial capital more easily and quickly than at any other point in human history.

These are only three reasons why we live in such a complex world. But how can you take these facts and apply them to your daily routine and the obstacles that you face every day?

The first step in moving toward your dreams is to change. How do you change? Quite simply, you create change. Yes, create it! How might this be so? A good analogy is an artist. An artist creates an image in his mind and allows the paint, brush, and technique to create his masterpiece. Don't be afraid to innovate. Be different. Following the herd is a sure way to mediocrity.

There are many examples of how a different view or perspective created an entirely new outlook. In history, we see examples of this as we study major paradigm shifts, when there is a major change in what constitutes the norm.

To really understand this approach, you must be willing to challenge and re-examine your existing paradigm. A paradigm is best described as the lens through which you perceive the world. For instance, the existing paradigm for many centuries was that the best way to govern was through the divine right of kings. A change in the paradigm occurred in the

United States when a democratic republic was established in which a written constitution institutionalized a system of principles that were not dependent on any one individual but on the ideals of democracy. Authority flowed from God to the people and then to the government, not just from God to the king. This approach allows the electorate to choose representatives who, in turn, make decisions on the people's behalf. This method is by no means perfect but our long lasting democracy has served as the model for other democratic nations.

With the advent of so many new forces interacting to accelerate the process, the magnitude of change has increased exponentially. Management guru Tom Peters points out how these paradigm shifts are becoming ever more frequent. Go back and examine our history. Around 1000 BC, a paradigm shift took about 1000 years: remember the Stone Age, Bronze Age, etc. By 1000 AD, it had sped up to about hundred years. More change took place in the century following 1800 than in the previous 900 years, and more change happened between 1900 and 1920 than in the entire previous century. In 2000, with the advent of the Internet, a dramatic paradigm shift is likely to occur every decade!

What does this all mean for us? It means we are entering a "no limits" era. Where the opportunity exists, it will happen. We are a "free agent nation". This term, coined by Daniel Pink, describes how all modern workers are "free agents" and define their own jobs. Yes, they still work around forty hours a week, but they get to decide which forty hours they will be.

So now you need to create the world that you want to live in. Do you want to be more in control of your destiny or do you want your destiny to control you? This is the fundamental question you must consider when evaluating the possibilities that confront you.

In order to achieve your dreams, you need to calculate how you will get there from here. Imagine this, when you go on a vacation, you don't just hop on an airplane. You map things out such as: Where am I going? Am I going to fly or drive? Where am I going to stay -- a Bed & Breakfast or a large chain hotel? Questions such as these apply to all areas of your life. Remember, things don't just happen; you made decisions and choices that led you to where you we now. You need to focus on a clear vision. Go back and review your beliefs. What do you stand for?

Clear Vision

What separates the winners and losers is vision. What do they see? Helen Keller was once asked if there was anything worse than being blind. She replied, "Yes, not having vision." Vision is the driving force propelling all successful people. They see where they are going and, better yet, they visualize being there. Focus your time and money; don't let other people or things distract you.

This is more than mere goal setting; it is a means to touch the future by creating vision today. Vision is a realistic, credible, attractive future for an individual. It is the individual's articulation of a destination toward which the individual or organization should aim. Vision is the primary vehicle by which you renew and direct yourself.

In simple terms, a vision is:

A dream or an ideal for what something could become.

An active imagination that allows you to glimpse how something could or should be.

A visual image of how an organization or individual would perform and how it would "look" if it were successful.

A signpost: it points the way for those who need to understand where you are going.

However, a vision can also disrupt the status quo, challenging what has long been accepted as "how things are." It may well be a "wake-up call" for the individual who needs fundamental change.

Everything you do is a "thought," acted upon and set into motion. No matter how small the thought may seem, it will ultimately have an affect on your life. Vision entails looking at your personal values and life purpose or how your life fits into a greater whole. This vision will give you POWER!! Yes, POWER!! It is the ultimate force of the universe; from being in a position of power and strength, your decisions will allow you to conquer the mountains ahead. You must believe in yourself before anyone else will. I know pundits who say that a poor self-esteem is a result of years of inner turmoil and conflict. Baloney! Individuals have poor self-esteem because they allow their self-doubt to control their ability to live. How do you overcome this destructive force? You tackle it head on, and you commit yourself to facing the danger. As in the arena, it is only then that the fighter knows his strengths and overcomes his weaknesses.

Clarify your focus - where am I going to do this? How is this going to help me get closer to my goals? The problem is never how to welcome new ideas into your mind, but how to evict the old ones. As history and life teaches, there is no free lunch.

Before anything will happen, you have to know what your desired outcome is. What do you want to happen? This is why goals are so important. Unfortunately, there is no magic formula or special pill you can take. It is simply a matter of sitting down and charting your course. Remember in Chapter 2, where you wrote down where you want to go in life? Use that as a starting point. Now all you have to do is develop a strategy to help you get there. Take that list and expand it, organizing it in the following categories:

Physical Goals

Intellectual Goals

Emotional Goals

Spiritual Goal

Why are these categories important and why is the order especially useful? First and foremost, you have to take care of your body; you have to make sure that you are giving it the right nutrition and exercise. You cannot do anything if you are sick. So write down your physical goals first. Ask yourself, what do you want to weigh, feel, or look like. Then explore your spiritual goals, because regardless of what religion or beliefs you hold true, you have to have a spiritual sense of value. It is the inner voice that defines the person you are.

How do you reflect and connect with the universe around you? How do you want to treat your friends and family? Do you want to develop new relationships with others or improve your communications with the people you care about? If this is the case, you need to focus on your personal goals.

What do you want to do with your life? How do you want to cultivate your mind and talents? What is your life's occupation? These questions will help you develop your professional goals. Finally, look at finances. Interestingly, most people usually list their financial goals first by stating, "I want to be rich." Yes, money is important because you have to pay rent, put food on the table and plan for a rainy day; however, you need balance in all areas of your life. Be specific; what level of economic security do you want for you and your family? Don't forget to plan for your retirement years or the possibility of bad health.

Physical goals:

Intellectual goals:

Emotional goals:

Spiritual goals:

Financial goals:

    Now that you have listed all the things you want to accomplish, write out the obstacles that are in the way of each. What has prevented you from attaining these goals? How will you overcome these limitations? Be as clear as you can and focus like a laser beam. Now that you know what you want and what is holding you back, develop a game plan. What steps will you take? What will you do this moment? What will you do every day from now on until you accomplish this goal? The key is to be as descriptive as you can. By writing it down, it forces you to think and clarify what you want. Lastly, give each of these goals a timeline that shows when you will reach them. Time is constantly moving forward and so must you.

    Now take these goals and paste them on your bathroom mirror, car dash, or TV set. Carry this list in your wallet or purse. Post them anywhere you will see them every day, several times a day. Only by reading them often and letting them enter your mind at the subconscious level will they become a part of you. Believe it and you can achieve it!! Keep a diary of your progress and reflect on what works and what does not work. Be flexible in your approach and focus on results; as an old Chinese proverb states,

"The branch that bends with the wind does not break."

Continue the Journey

You have been sent on a journey called life. There are rules that apply to this journey, but you've had to learn them as you go along and you can't control them. You may not even know the purpose of the journey, even though others may claim to. All you know is that once started you must continue every day, whether you feel like it or not. You start with no possessions and when you finish you must turn in all that you have accumulated. In the end, some believe you will be punished or rewarded. But how do they know for sure? When it's all said and done, all you have left is a chronicle of the journey.

We have all embarked on a journey, and it will be over before we know it. Stop thinking along the same old well-worn track, and broaden your perspective to encompass the world and the universe. We live in a time that makes the impossible possible. Think about it: we are better off today than the richest man in the world was 100 years ago. You can travel across the planet in less than a day. You can communicate with anyone, anywhere and hear their voice as clearly as if they were standing next to you. Be grateful for every day and love life. Become a life experiencer and continual learner. Focus on a brighter future and don't stop thinking about tomorrow.

ABC Vision

Remember these simple rules of happiness to live by:

Free your heart from hatred

> Free your mind from worry
>
> Live simply
>
> Give more
>
> Expect less

Keep life in perspective: don't worry about the small stuff and realize that everything is small. Ask yourself, will the planet keep turning? If so, you can overcome whatever blip appears on the screen. Continue to be a life-long learner and live life with passion.

FIVE The Final Word - SUCCESS!!

Go For the Max! Be all you can be! Shoot your best shot! Live life to the fullest!
-Max Cleland, former United States Senator (D-GA)

    I asked Jack Welch, former head of General Electric, "How do you become successful?" He responded, "Quite simply, live your life's passion. Only you can determine your own level of success in life, be it as an artist, a teacher, or business person." This book began with a promise to open up a new world of opportunity for you and we end with the same promise. In all of human history, every person who walked on this planet has experienced the same things you have: the physical, spiritual, and emotional dimensions of the mortal existence. You have hidden treasures within you, and you need to discover these jewels. The three basic principles of success, which are your Attitude, Beliefs, and Commitment, serve as the beginning of your journey toward your dreams. The ABC Vision method was created to help capture the wisdom of the ages. As we conclude this book, the most challenging part of this simple method is to focus on applying these principles each and every day.

    This approach is not a cure-all, but a method you can use to help you shape your own destiny. Life is not easy; it is tough, but you are tougher. Only you can choose to make your life better or worse. Today is a new day, so permit yourself to get closer to your dreams. Continuous learning is vital in order to be able to excel in our complex world. In today's information-based environment, knowledge is the key that opens many locked doors of opportunity. The constant battle is not finding new ideas, but getting rid of the old ideas blocking the way and making room for the new ones. Stay open to new ideas and be flexible. As Einstein said, "The more I learn, the less I know." The basic definition of learning is to he able to modify one's behavior in response to given external factors. Learn to love learning and seek new ideas by listening to others. There is a Zen saying, "When the student is ready, the teacher will appear."

You are not alone. Every problem that you face today has been dealt with by others in the past, is being experienced by others in the present, and will confront others in the future. Seek answers by tackling life's questions. Goethe put this into perspective when he said, "Man is not born to solve the problems of the universe, but to find out what he has to do."

Let's review. Everyone has one thing in common – their problems. Don't we all fret about not having enough money, time, and/or love? Every day is filled with triumphs and tragedies. Once you realize that problems are part of all our daily lives, you can then focus on the solutions. Decide to change your current situation into the life that you desire. Use your energy wisely; don't confuse activities with accomplishments. At the end of the day, the results are what count.

The wisdom in this book is useless unless you are open to shifting your course. The best time to act is today, so start anew, time is ticking away. As Ben

Franklin was fond of saying, "Lost time is never found again." So don't count your days, but make your days count. Keep on reminding yourself that your life begins now. Dare to soar and live with passion.

Attitude = Vision Where do you want to go?

Every day you face new challenges and obstacle. The only way you can overcome them is to determine the attitude you will have. This means that what you feed your mind determines the person you become. Simple. Think of this as a simple equation negative in equals negative out, positive in equals positive out. You, and you alone, can control what your mind accepts or rejects. Good attitudes are contagious; is yours worth catching?

Life is not your enemy, but your thinking can be. By controlling your thoughts you can control your outcome. Accept responsibility for your present state. It will free you from blaming others for the situation that you find yourself in.

What are your dreams? Now that you have taken responsibility, make an honest assessment of your life and pinpoint where you stand. Review what you are grateful for and what is in your control that can or will make you happy.

Finally, and crucially, take action in seeking a means of attaining what you want. Create a vision of where you want to go. Concentrate on listening, to the inner voice of truth and it will never lead you astray.

Dr. Wilson L. Triviño @abcvision

Beliefs = Core Values Why do I want to do this?

Take the first step and become determined to live the dream and seek the inner power to do so. Your beliefs are the core of your being. They determine your actions and reactions. Believe in yourself and remember that you are an original You are in control. No one can make you feel inferior unless you let them do so. Break free from the limitations of the past. Don't ever underestimate your power to make a difference. Climb to new heights and discover the awesome view!

Concentrate on your beliefs and review your personal mission statement. Repeat it over and over. Let this message keep you on course.

Commitment = focus = How will I get there?

Choose to live life today. Your commitment is your focus and will determine how you will get to your destination. How do you cut down an oak tree? You don't cut it down by sawing it off at the trunk, but by cutting one branch at a time. That makes it manageable and systematically possible to cart the tree away. This simple principle also applies to life; one step at a time moves you toward your destination.

Change is inevitable. Accept continual change and change before you have to. No one can change until they really want to change. Constantly grow and evolve into a more potent individual. Stephen Covey speaks to the key of life, "Between stimulus and response, there is a space. In that space, lies our freedom and power to choose our response. In those choices will lay our growth and happiness."

Create a clear vision. You can have the life you want, but you have to know your destination in advance and desire it with all your heart. Write down your goals and outline the steps needed to reach them. Without a definite goal and a plan of action to achieve it, you cannot reach your destination. Be committed to change and handle the daily challenges of life. Realize that if it's going to be, it's up to you. You are the only one who can determine the outcome of your personal story. Think of the laws of the harvest: farmers do not procrastinate; they must get out and plant the seeds, work the land, and then reap the benefits of their labor. In life, as in farming, you cannot cram the night before and expect to reap a good harvest. How can you enjoy your goals of tomorrow, if you don't work toward them today? Know where you are going and focus on the finish line. Be committed to your goals, for without discipline, you can do nothing in this world, nothing! No matter what happens, always, always remember that the past is fact, the present is reality, and the future is possibility. Continue the journey by moving forward.

Conclusion

The powerful messages in this book are not new, but they are timeless. As the end of the book nears, you need to ingrain the power of ABC in your conscious and unconscious mind. Your Attitude, Beliefs, and Commitment are the keys to unlocking the mystery of your dreams. Think outside the box, be proactive and try something new. Live as the saying instructs: "Dance like nobody is watching, love like you've never been hurt, and work like you're not being paid." Like a music box, let the music from within fill the air with rhythm, spirit, and soul.

Life is difficult, but you are strong. Martin Luther King, Jr. proclaimed, "The ultimate measure of a man is not where he stands in moments of comfort and convenience, but where he stands at times of challenge and controversy." Things will happen, people will disappoint you, and problems may arise. These are only part of life's test. Know that a bend in the road is not the end of the road, unless you fail to make the turn. Even through our tears, there are opportunities to envision. Seek that opening! I cannot stress this enough, because every problem has a solution.

Have a higher purpose in living. Happiness and success are the results of purpose and productive living rather than the outcome. Your life's meaning is a by-product of reaching beyond yourself and helping others help themselves. Focus beyond yourself. Service to others is the rent we pay for living. Mother Theresa believed that "life is a promise; fulfill it!"

Even if you are able to reach the level of success that you have always sought, don't stop growing and reaching toward new challenges. As Robert Browning said, "Ah, but a man's reach should exceed his grasp, or what's heaven for?" Become a life experiencer and continue to expand your world of wonder.

Finally, what is your legacy? What imprints will remain after you are gone from this mortal world? How will your presence change humanity and make the planet a better place than you found it? Within the next twenty-four hours, share the ABC method, your Attitude, Beliefs, and Commitment, with someone you know and by teaching you will learn the material twice. More importantly, you might help someone else help him or herself. You can be whatever you make up your mind to be. What's in your mind is all that counts. At the end of the day, the only people who fail are those that do not try. So just do it!

Focus on today, because yesterday is gone, tomorrow is not guaranteed and today is a gift from the present.

I have saved my best story for last. I was fortunate enough to have the opportunity to meet the former heavy weight champion of the world, Muhammad Ali, and I told him, "Champ you are the greatest!" His dancing eyes focused on me and he responded, "The greatest of all time." What a powerful belief in oneself. I am here to tell you that you too are the greatest of all time. No one exactly like you will ever exist on this planet and you should live each day as if it were your last. Control your destiny or someone else will. Use the ABC Vision winning formula and become a SUCCESS by living the life YOU want to lead!

Dr. Wilson L. Triviño @abcvision

REFERENCES

Bennis, Warren and Burt Nanus. *1985*. Leaders: The Strategies For Taking Charge. New York: NY: Harper Row.

Carlson, Richard. 1997. You Can Be Happy No Matter What. Novato, CA:
New World Library.

Carnegie, Dale. 1984. How to Stop Worrying and Start Living. New York, NY: Simon and Schuster.
Chaffee, John. 1998. The Thinker's Way: 8 Steps to a Richer Life. Boston, MA: Little, Brown, and Company.

Cleland, Max. 1999. Going for The Max: 12 Principles for Living Life to the Fullest. Nashville, TN: Broadman & Holman Publisher.

Cleland, Max. 2000. Strong at the Broken Places. Marietta, GA: Longstreet Press.

Covey, Stephen R. 1990. The 7 Habits of Highly Effective People. New York, NY: Simon & Schuster, Dalai Lama and Howard C. Cutler. 1998. The Art of Happiness. New York, NY: Penguin Books.

Dyer, Wayne W. 1989. You've Seen It When You Believe It. New York: NY: Avon Books.

Dyer, Wayne. W. 1992. Real Magic: Creating Miracles in Everyday Life. New York, NY: Harper Books.

Dyer, Wayne W. 1998. Wisdom of the Ages. New York, NY: Harper Collins Books.

Eitel, Charlie. 1995. Eitel Time: Turnaround Secrets. Orlando, FL: Harcourt Brace & Company.

Ford, Debbie. 1998. The Dark Side of the Light Chasers. New York, NY: Riverhead Books.

Larkin, Willie D. 1998. Choose Not To be Average Strive to he Great!!!. Auburn, AL:Cotton Patch Publishing.

Loeb, Paul Rogat. 1999. Soul of A Citizen: Living With Conviction in A Cynical Time. New York, NY: St. Martin Press.

Mackey, Harvey. 1990. Dig Your Well Before You're Thirsty. New York, NY: Bantam Doubleday Publishing Group.

Ortberg, John 0. 1997. The Life You've Always Wanted. Grand Rapids, MI: Zondervan Publishing House.

Peale, Norman Vincent. *1953*. The Power of Positive Thinking. New York, NY: Prentice-Hall, Inc.

Peters, Tom and Robert H. Waterman. 1982. In Search of Excellence. New York: NY: Harper & Row.

Pink, Daniel H. 2001. Free Agent Nation: How America's New Independent Workers Are Transforming the Way We Live. New York, NY: Warner Books, Inc.

Reich, Robert. 2001. The Future of Success. New York, NY: Random House.

Reiman, Joey. 1998. Thinking For A Living. Marietta, GA: Longstreet.

Robbins, Anthony. 1991. <u>Awaken the Giant Within.</u> New York, NY:
Fireside Books.

Schuller Robert H. 1987. <u>The Be (Happy) Attitudes.</u> Irving, TX: Bantam Books.

Schuller Robert H. 1993. <u>Power Thoughts: Achieve Your True Potential Through Thinking.</u> New York, NY: Harper Paper Back Books.

Ziglar, Zig. 1994. <u>Over The Top: Moving from Survival To Stability, from Stability to Success, from Success to Significance.</u> Nashville, TN: Thomas Nelson, Inc.

Ziglar, Zig. 1999. <u>Something Else to Smile About.</u> Nashville, TN: Thomas Nelson, Inc.

ABOUT THE AUTHOR

Political Scientist Dr. Wilson L. Triviño is speaker, writer, and entrepreneur.

Since January 2011, he has read over 1700 books and written over 1000 book reviews. He speaks on change, pop culture, technology, politics, and sex. A futurist with a love of fountain pens and vintage typewriters.

Triviño was the first Latino to receive a doctorate in Public Policy and Public Administration from Auburn University in Auburn, Alabama. He holds a Masters in Public Administration from Auburn University and a Bachelor of Arts from Kennesaw State University.

Dr. Wilson L. Triviño has a daily live stream show that broadcasts about ideas, reviews cool products and cultural events on Periscope and Meerkat (@abcvision). He is a social media guru and content creator that is available on multiple platforms

He resides in Atlanta, Georgia and is dedicated entrepreneur creating positive change every day. Read his column at www.PurePolitics.com Follow him @abcvision on Meerkat/Periscope/Instagram/Twitter – If you see him IRL (in real life), please come up and say hello. Check out his YouTube channel @T4Vista

If you would like to interview Dr. Wilson L. Triviño, book to speak at your next event, or review a product or a cool social occasion, contact him at Twitter/ Instagram - @abcvision /abcvision@hotmail.com

www.ingramcontent.com/pod-product-compliance
Lightning Source LLC
Chambersburg PA
CBHW032212040426
42449CB00005B/551